PANDEMIC

REFLECTIONS ON COVID-19, GOD'S SOVEREIGNTY, CHURCH, & MISSION

BY STEVEN R. MARTINS

THE CÁNTARO  MONOGRAPHS

cp

cántaro
publications

www.cantaroinstitute.org

Published by Cántaro Publications, a publishing imprint of the Cántaro Institute, Jordan Station, ON.

Book design by Steven R. Martins

Library & Archives Canada

ISBN 978-1-7772356-3-5

About the Cántaro Institute

Inheriting, Informing, Inspiring

The Cántaro Institute is a confessional evangelical Christian organization established in 2020 that seeks to recover the riches of Spanish Protestantism for the renewal and edification of the contemporary church and to advance the comprehensive Christian philosophy of life for the religious reformation of the Western and Ibero-American world.

We believe that as the Christian church returns to the fount of Scripture as her ultimate authority for all knowing and living, and wisely applies God's truth to every aspect of life, faithful in spirit to the reformers, her missiological activity will result in not only the renewal of the human person but also the reformation of culture, an inevitable result when the true scope and nature of the gospel is made known and applied.

CONTENTS

PANDEMIC

REFLECTIONS ON COVID-19, GOD'S SOVEREIGNTY, CHURCH, & MISSION

PANDEMONIUM

THOUGH WE MAY TIRE of hearing the phrase, it nonetheless remains true: We have been living in *unprecedented* times. Not since the 1918 Spanish flu had there been such a disruption to societal life in the West like that which we have experienced with COVID-19. I can vividly recall when, on March 11, 2020, the National Basketball Association (NBA) suspended its season after one of its players tested positive for the virus. Though the Toronto Raptors' time as reigning champions was extended – after all, who could challenge them if there was no basketball to play? – the alarming news of COVID-19's arrival hit North American markets hard.[1]

---

1. Sam Quinn, "Coronavirus: NBA commissioner Adam Silver says league will wait at least 30 days before continuing season", *CBS Sports*. Accessed March 16, 2020, https://www.cbssports.com/nba/news/coronavirus-nba-commissioner-adam-silver-says-league-will-wait-at-least-30-days-before-continuing-season/.

The National Hockey League (NHL), Major League Baseball (MLB), and several other high-profile sports leagues shortly followed suit.[2] In order to understand the significance of these big-league suspensions, fiscally, we are talking about a multi-million(billion?)-dollar loss in the sports industry, that is *no insignificant* number. And to think that these suspensions were only the beginning of COVID-19's impact on North America. Stocks began to freefall, a global recession was accelerated, Canada and the United States closed its borders to non-essential travelers, Ottawa's House of Commons suspended its operations, public schools across the country moved to online learning, university campuses shut down, workplaces sent their employees home, and grocery stores like Costco, NoFrills and Walmart were stripped bare in the first few weeks of the nation-wide lockdown. All this and more had developed in a short matter of time with COVID-19's arrival. With all the panic and the hysteria that comes with the word "pandemic", Western society had been thrown into utter pandemonium.

For those who had been following the news, the writing was on the wall. The impact of COVID-19 was first witnessed in Wuhan, China, eventually extending to the rest of the country, and then the rest of Asia. Iran soon followed, which was one of the hardest

2. Gabriel Fernandez, "Coronavirus live updates: NBA, MLB, other U.S. sports pause as CDC recommends 8 week stop for large gatherings", *CBS Sports*. Accessed March 16, 2020, https://www.cbssports.com/general/news/coronavirus-live-updates-nba-mlb-other-u-s-sports-pause-as-cdc-recommends-8-week-stop-for-large-gatherings/live/.

hit countries in the Middle East. Europe was neither spared from the pandemic, and was considered the epicenter for a time before shifting to the Americas. Countries like Italy and Brazil had struggled to deal with the virus' breakout, and had even been forced to turn people away from hospitals due to the lack of space, beds, and resources. As per the words of Tedros A. Ghebreyesus in the early days of the pandemic, the Director-General of the WHO:

> We expect[ed] to see the number of cases, the number of deaths, and the number of affected countries climb even higher... We have never before seen a pandemic sparked by a coronavirus. This is the first pandemic caused by a coronavirus.[3]

After some careful reflection, the panic and hysteria was not altogether unexpected, if anything, this was in part (and only in part) a healthy response to an alarming threat. In 1918 the pandemic of the Spanish flu ravaged most of the world, at the time one third of earth's population was infected, and 20-50 million people are estimated to have died. In 1956 there was the Asian Flu by which, according to the WHO, 2 million people are estimated to have died. And in 1968, the Flu Pandemic killed little more than a million people. Pandemics are not new, they have occurred numerous times in the past.[4] The most recent scare in the West,

3. World Health Organization, "Rolling updates on coronavirus disease (COVID-19)", *WHO*. Accessed March 16, 2020, https://www.who.int/emergencies/diseases/novel-coronavirus-2019/events-as-they-happen/.

4. "Worst Pandemics in History", *MPHonline*. Accessed March 16, 2020, https://www.mphonline.org/worst-pandemics-in-history/.

prior to COVID-19, was SARS (Severe Acute Respiratory Syndrome), which emerged in 2002 and 2003 as a species of the coronavirus. While SARS managed to cross oceans and devastated many, it never met the necessary conditions to be declared a "pandemic", and given its mortality rate of 10%, we should all be thankful for that fact.[5] That was in large part thanks to the medical professionals who worked day and night to contain the virus and treat its patients, some of which gave their lives to the cause.

SARS was an "epidemic", medically defined as an:

> occurrence of more cases of a disease or illness than expected in a given community or region or among a specific group of people over a particular period of time; a wave of infections in a region by an organism with a short generation time; epidemics are usually heralded by an exponential rise in number of cases in time and a decline as susceptible persons are exhausted.[6]

COVID-19, or SARS Covid-2, was declared on March 11, 2020 by the World Health Organization (WHO) to be a "pandemic." What is a pandemic? Medically speaking, it is "an epidemic (a sudden outbreak) that becomes very widespread and affects a whole region, a continent, or the world due to a susceptible

5. Mark Abadi, Havovi Cooper and Meg Teckman-Fullard, "How the coronavirus compares to SARS, swine flu, Zika, and other epidemics", *Business Insider.* Accessed March 16, 2020, https://www.businessinsider.com/coronavirus-compared-to-sars-swine-flu-mers-zika-2020-3/.

6. *McGraw-Hill Concise Dictionary of Modern Medicine* (The McGraw-Hill Companies, 2002).

population."[7] COVID-19 has demonstrated itself to be a *global* epidemic, a *pan*demic.

The Facts of COVID-19

Here were the facts related to COVID-19 as of March 11, 2020, communicated by infectious disease expert and Christian church leader Miguel Núñez:

> This virus has spread to more than 115 nations. As of March 11, there are more than 126,300 cases reported in the infected countries. Of these, some 68,285 patients have fully recovered, there are about 53,382 cases considered active, and more than 4,633 people have died.[8]

While China had seen a significant drop in cases of the coronavirus, in large part due to its extreme measures to contain it, Europe was climbing towards its pique, evidencing a more severe impact than witnessed in Asia – and the Americas were not far behind. The rapid growth and spread was to be expected, and both Canada and the US braced for its impact. As Canadian medical experts predicted, as of March 16, 2020:

> The coronavirus could hit 35 to 70 per cent of the Canadian population, making "a huge number of people ill," many critically, and makeshift hospitals and quaran-

7.   William C. Shiel Jr., "Medical Definition of Pandemic", *MedicineNet*. Accessed March 16, 2020, https://www.medicinenet.com/script/main/art.asp?articlekey=4751/.

8.   Miguel Núñez, "The FAQs: Coronavirus Explained by an Infectious Disease Expert and Pastor", *TGC*. Accessed March 16, 2020, https://www.thegospelcoalition.org/article/what-we-know-coronavirus/.

tine centres could be needed to shore up a health system that has virtually no give…[9]

Additionally, Canada's top health officer, Dr. Theresa Tam, commented that:

Our window to flatten the curve of the epidemic is narrow… We all need to act now. COVID-19 is a serious public health threat…[10]

The messaging had been similar to what was being communicated south of the border and even further south in Latin America.

It was not, however, all doom and gloom. There was good news that the media were not as ready to communicate (What sells stories more? Positivity or negativity?): The mortality rate was not as high as SARS. In fact, the average mortality rate was around 3.4%. Núñez wrote back in March 2020 that the "highest-risk patients are those older than 60 and those who suffer from a chronic disease, either respiratory or another type such as diabetes mellitus or renal failure."[11] This meant that, if you were under 60, and you did not have any chronic disease, then you *should* be able

9. Sharon Kirkey, "Coronavirus could infect 35 to 70 per cent of Canadians, expert says", *National Post*. Accessed March 16, 2020, https://nationalpost.com/news/canada/coronavirus-could-infect-35-to-70-per-cent-of-canadian-population-experts-say/.

10. Michelle McQuigge, "Our window to flatten the COVID-19 curve is narrow, says Dr. Theresa Tam", *CTV News*. Accessed March 16, 2020, https://www.ctvnews.ca/health/coronavirus/our-window-to-flatten-the-covid-19-curve-is-narrow-says-dr-theresa-tam-1.4853951/.

11. Núñez, "The FAQs: Coronavirus Explained by an Infectious Disease Expert and Pastor".

Figure 1: International statistics of Coronavirus COVID-19 cases as of March 13, 2020, 9:39am. Tracking of COVID-19 cases and deaths is available at "Coronavirus Map", *New York Times*. Accessed July 30, 2020. https://www.nytimes.com/interactive/2020/world/coronavirus-maps.html/.; Free image license from Pexels.

to weather this pandemic – there are, of course, exceptions. In fact, there had been several asymptomatic cases reported. Still, while a 3.4% mortality rate is not considered "high", it did not diminish the danger that this posed to the "high-risk." The elderly and the chronically-ill matter just as much as children and young healthy adults,[12] they are *not* by any means insignificant, they too are created in the *imago Dei*.

Even if you were not part of that "high-risk" group, however, the question remained: Who really wanted to get sick anyway? Or risk spreading the virus to loved ones or neighbours, particularly if they *were* "high-risk"? My father, for example, who was undergoing chemotherapy and who also happens to be diabetic, had a compromised immune system and was considered "high-risk". My advice to him had been to stay inside, to wash his hands, to limit or restrict his visitors. I wanted him to be safe. I wanted everyone to be safe, especially those who were "high-risk." I am not by any means a medical doctor, a healthcare provider, or a virologist, and I will not pretend to be an expert on COVID-19. However, based on what we had been hearing from the WHO, the CDC, and Canada's Public Health, it was clear that we all needed to be doing all that we could, including social distancing, in order to slow the spread of COVID-19. All the official infor-

---

12. It was reported after the first COVID-19 wave that children were at risk too, see Amanda Ghosh, "Emerging COVID-19 complications in children", *MultiBriefs Exclusive*. Accessed July 22, 2020, https://exclusive.multibriefs.com/content/emerging-covid-19-complications-in-children/science-technology/.

mation related to preparation, prevention, risk, symptoms, treatment, and travel advice, had been made easily accessible by means of the Government of Canada's Public Health website[13] and that of the Centers for Disease Control and Prevention.[14] In many respects, the general populace were far more better informed and prepared than in other places of the world.

The church, unfortunately, was not *un*affected by all this. It too was subject to the nation-wide lockdown. However, with the forced cancellation of weekly church services – and this was due to a restriction of gatherings from initially 250 to then 5 people for a period of 11 weeks – there was ample enough time for the church, the body of Christ, to contemplate the world's events and to meditate on the counsels of Scripture. Given all that had transpired, and in the midst of all the cultural confusion, there were three biblical facts that I had endeavoured to communicate to our congregation at Sevilla Chapel, facts that were relevant to these unprecedented times. These were: (1) God is still sovereign; (2) The world needs the gospel; and (3) The institutional church is still important. These remain true, even today.

---

13. See Government of Canada, "Coronavirus disease (COVID-19)", *Canada.* Accessed March 16, 2020, https://www.canada.ca/en/public-health/services/diseases/coronavirus-disease-covid-19.html/.

14. See Centers for Disease Control and Prevention, "Coronavirus (COVID-19)", *CDC.* Accessed March 16, 2020, https://www.cdc.gov/coronavirus/2019-nCoV/index.html/.

1. God is still Sovereign

Yes, it is true. God is still sovereign. He is in control of *all* things in spite of what we might see in the world. And just as God is *sovereign*, so is He also *good*. This is what we can understand from God's self-disclosing revelation:

> Whatever the LORD pleases, he does,
>> in heaven and on earth,
>> in the seas and all deeps (Ps. 135:6).

> Remember the former things of old;
>> for I am God, and there is no other;
>> I am God, and there is none like me,
> declaring the end from the beginning
>> and from ancient times things not yet done,
> saying, "My counsel shall stand,
>> and I will accomplish all my purpose"
>> (Isa. 46:9-10).

> And he said, "I will make all my goodness pass before you and will proclaim before you my name 'The LORD.' And I will be gracious to whom I will be gracious, and will show mercy on whom I will show mercy (Exod. 33:19).

> Oh, taste and see that the LORD is good!
>> Blessed is the man who takes refuge in him!
>> (Ps. 34:8).

If God is sovereign, and if God is good, as Scripture teaches, then logically He has a *morally sufficient reason* for why He has allowed COVID-19 to exist – just as He has a *morally sufficient reason* for the (temporary) existence of evil and suffering. We may not understand it ourselves, after all, we are *in* time and space, we are *in* this fallen world, we are *subject* to the fallenness, but God in His infinite wisdom knows the why behind it all, and one day, perhaps from eternity, we will come to understand the "why".

What might possibly come to mind is the hand of God's judgment, and we would not be far off to consider that possibility. King David, for example, in 1 Chronicles 21, witnessed God's hand of judgment by means of a plague when he had put forth the order for a census. Verse 14 reads "So the Lord sent a pestilence on Israel, and 70,000 men of Israel fell." While a census is not sinful in and of itself, the *intention* by which David ordered the census was. It was an attempt to compare his military might to other nations, it was to accredit the grandeur of Israel to David's mighty army and his governance over them. As one biblical commentator wrote: "Why was God displeased with it? David's purpose was to assess his military strength in *humanistic* terms."[15] David's sin was the sin of pride, the sin that vainly attempts to rob God of His rightful glory. It is likely that the prophet Gad confronted David over this sin, for it is Gad who communicates God's judgment; similar to how the prophet Nathan confronted David over his sin with Bathsheba (2 Sam. 12:7-14). The historical narrative records David's response as throwing himself before the Lord in repentance, and because of that, he and the kingdom are

---

15. R.J, Rushdoony, *Numbers: Volume IV of Commentaries on the Pentateuch* (Chalcedon Foundation, 2009), Kindle edition.

spared from total destruction (1 Chron. 21:15-17), but the *consequence* of the sin followed nonetheless. God would bring about the humiliation of Israel, by means of a pestilence, because of the king's foolishness. Here we read the very real biblical principle of God judging nations, *not only* for what the people do, but for what their *leaders* do as well. Even having considered this biblical passage, however, we cannot say with certainty that this is the case with COVID-19, that is, that the hand of God's judgment has come upon man in this form because of the mounting sin of the apostasized Western nations. Perhaps it has (it aligns, after all, with Scriptural truth), or perhaps it has not (there may be another reason that God has in mind). That has not been revealed to us, however. At best we can infer, speculate even, but ultimately God knows the reason *why*.

Job, during the time of his testing and suffering, after having been awe-struck by the power and wonder of God, realized that even if God were to have provided the why behind his suffering, he would not have understood it in the slightest. As Job said, "...I have uttered what I did not understand, things too wonderful for me, which I did not know" (Job 42:3). As Bible commentator R.L. Alden states, "[Job] had spoken out of ignorance of things that were beyond his ability to understand (Ps. 131:1). It is a charge that would indict us all."[16] What we know from God's special revelation, the Bible, is more than sufficient, for *He* has deemed it

---

16. R.L. Alden, *The New American Commentary: Vol. 11, Job* (Nashville: Broadman & Holman Publishers, 1993), 408.

sufficient. It is the only authoritative interpretation of God's revelation in creation. And what is made most clear to us, by the unified revelation of Scripture and creation, is that we live in a sin-cursed world.

In light of that fact, it is by presupposing the biblical truths of God's sovereignty and goodness that we can take to heart what J.C. Ryle wrote in response to an outbreak of cholera in 1866:

> Vestries may fail to do their duty, and Governments may be slow to act. Hospitals may be overcrowded, and doctors may fail. But the Lord reigns and we have no cause to despair… This is the Lord's hand – let us take comfort. The hand that made the world is too wise to err. The hand that was nailed to the cross is too loving to lay on us more than we can bear. Cholera is an enemy that can do no more than God is pleased to allow.[17]

We could rephrase those last words of Ryle to say: "**COVID-19** is an enemy that can do no more than God is pleased to allow."

While panic and hysteria are to be expected during pandemics, as followers of Christ, we are *not* to be panic-stricken during such times. We are to be counter-cultural in this regard as well, as the salt and light of the earth. We have the privilege of knowing that our good and sovereign God holds all things in His hands. We may not understand the why, and that is okay, for as God said through the prophet Isaiah:

> For my thoughts are not your thoughts,
> 　　neither are your ways my ways,

---

17. J.C. Ryle, *"The Hand of the Lord!" Being Thoughts on Cholera* (London: William Hunt, 1865).

> declares the LORD.
> For as the heavens are higher than the earth,
>> so are my ways higher than your ways
>> and my thoughts than your thoughts (Isa. 55:8-9).

What we *do* however know from God's self-revelation is that God is good and He is sovereign, and we must have faith that He who provided the means for our salvation at great cost to Himself is the same who will bring about the eventual restoration of all creation. He will be glorified, and we shall partake in that glory if we trust in Him wholeheartedly. Evil and suffering will be brought to an end once and for all according to His appointed time (1 Cor. 15:24-26). It is *this* hope, the hope of the gospel, that *comprehensive* gospel, that must be evident in our daily witness, especially during a pandemic.

2. The World Needs the Gospel

And witness we must, for what greater opportunity is there to bear witness of the gospel than during a time when so many people are panic-stricken and hysterical because of their fear of death? Why else would people panic? Because food on store shelves might suddenly disappear? Canada and the US have such intricately advanced supply systems that such a prospect is more fantasy than reality. No, the fear that resides in fallen man's heart is *death*. Such a fear is unnatural when we consider that mankind was not created to die but to live forever in the presence and fellowship of God. And yet we fear it because it is a reality, a saddening memory of the sin of our first parents, of our *own* sin, for the "wages of sin is death" (Rom. 6:23).

Before all the pandemonium, before COVID-19 came onto the scene, the natural (that is to say, unregenerate) man was so confident in his self-sufficiency, in his scientific proficiency, of his lordship over creation, that he deemed the God of the Bible as unnecessary and thus non-existential. It is the pride of sinful man that has been on full display in the West ever since society's departure from Christendom, it is a pride as ancient as our first parents. But such pride falls on its face, as Scripture teaches: "Pride goes before destruction, and a haughty spirit before a fall" (Prov. 16:18). On this matter, the renowned theologian Herman Bavinck stated:

> One moment man considers himself infinitely superior to nature and believes it no longer has any secrets for him. The next moment [it] is a dark and mysterious power he does not understand, whose riddles he cannot solve, and from whose power he cannot free himself.[18]

By discarding the God of the Bible, by renouncing God's truths and His special revelation, by suppressing the truth revealed through creation, man in his sinfulness has turned to the sciences, not in an effort to understand the world for what it is, but to deify himself, to take the place of God, and to govern creation with god-like powers. As the Dutch Christian philosopher Herman Dooyeweerd had stated:

> Science, secularized and isolated, has become a satanic power, an idol which dominates all of culture... sec-

---

18. Herman Bavinck, *Reformed Dogmatics, Vol. 2: God and Creation* (Grand Rapids, MI.: Baker Academic, 2004), 438.

ularized science has never ceased to be the dominating force in Occidental culture. Quite the contrary! Its power has been enhanced to an astonishing degree as it has given rise to unheard-of technological advances. It is an impersonal power which has rationalized all of society. Even if it is no longer venerated as a goddess, it can nevertheless manifest itself as a demon, impressing on man's soul the theoretical image of reality which it has created, an image which cannot be squared with the Christian faith.[19]

What the natural man seeks is control over nature, not to the degree of being able to control it, but beyond that, to the extent of being able to create his own reality. To best articulate it, the natural man seeks to control creation and to turn it into what it is not. Our first parents sought total control when they ate from the forbidden tree, they sought total independence from God, but that "control" has been shown to be a farce. Man might be deceived into thinking that we can be the masters of our own destiny, that we can be the masters of created reality, but that lie has been exposed for what it is by the COVID-19 pandemic. We *fear* death because we *cannot control* death. All of man's activities in the playground of the empirical sciences, to be more specific, the secularized and isolated sciences, has made man think that he can *control* nature as a God-substitute, but this could not be any further from the truth.

COVID-19 has served as a sober reminder that man is *not* in control of all things, no matter how confi-

---

19. Herman Dooyeweerd, *The Secularization of Science* (Jordan Station, ON.: Paideia Press, 2020), 6, 8.

dent he might be in his own pretended self-sufficiency, no matter how proficient he may become in the disciplines of the sciences, no matter what he may build or establish in society, *he is no lord.* There is only *one* Lord, *one* King over all creation, the sinless God-man, Jesus Christ. It is in such present cultural conditions that man must hear the gospel, for only then can he find comfort in the face of death, and joy in spite of the brokenness and futility of our fallen world. As the theologian Willem J. Ouweneel has written:

> There are three things you must know if you would know the joy and comfort of belonging to Jesus Christ. First, you have to realize that you need to be saved because you are a prisoner of the power of sin, death and the devil. Second, you have to know the way out of this spiritual captivity. Third, you have to learn how to live once you have received your salvation.[20]

The way out of man's spiritual captivity is by means of (i) repentance and (ii) faith in the Son of God. God has called the church for such a time as this, to be bold and intentional in our witness of the gospel. For from the gospel comes redemption and renewal, and a right understanding of all things from God's inscripturated revelation.

Of course, questions have abounded given the unique challenges of the pandemic. Principally concerning the "How?" When the social distancing guidelines are taken into consideration (guidelines that may remain in effect for a few months to potentially years),

---

20. Willem J. Ouweneel, *The Heidelberg Diary: Daily Devotions on the Heidelberg Catechism* (Jordan Station, ON.: Paideia Press, 2018), 6.

it is clear that sharing the gospel with our neighbour, bearing witness as to the truth of the Christian worldview, is not as "easy" as it used to be. No matter how one might look at it, however, the challenge is not as daunting as one might think. All that may be required is a bit of outside-of-the-box creativity, breaking out of our modern traditional norms. A few churches in Niagara, for example, offered to purchase and deliver food for the elderly and other "high-risk" persons. Something which we have seen across the country as well. Such a demonstration of love and concern for the well-being of our neighbours is consistent with what Scripture teaches, but it cannot go *un*accompanied by the proclamation of the gospel. The gospel message establishes the context of our missional service. We are not serving others merely for the sake of it, nor because it simply makes us feel better – we are serving others because One who is far greater than us came to serve us sacrificially. The words of Christ should spring to mind: "…the Son of Man came not to be served but to serve, and to give his life as a ransom for many" (Matt. 20:28). It is only from the Christian worldview that can we make sense of charity and good-will to men.

Consider, also, that social distancing does not mean total isolation or exile, as if no fellowship or conversation can be had, whether over a short distance, on the phone, or via video-conferencing. I have always found that when we ask God for opportunities to share the gospel, He provides those opportunities. Was it not Paul who said "…pray also for us, that God may open to us a door for the word, to declare the mystery of Christ…" (Col. 4:3)? Consider China, for example, where the church has been aggressively suppressed by the state. Christians have been shown to be preaching the gospel and handing out tracts and Bibles to pass-ersby on the streets while dressed in protective medical gear.[21] They have no fear, either of the coronavirus or of the state, or at least, fear does not *dominate* them.[22] Why might that be? Because death is not the end for those who trust in Jesus. And what the state can ulti-mately do is little compared to what God can do. What we see in China is a church that does not fear man, a church that instead has a high reverential fear of God, such is the beginning of wisdom (Prov. 9:10). These brothers and sisters in the faith are faithfully embody-ing their Christian hope as they live "sent out" into the world. While what we may do may look a bit differ-ent considering our context, we should nonetheless be encouraged and emboldened to reach out and engage with our own communities.

21. See Emma Williamson, "Christians at the Centre of Coronavirus Outbreak still Preaching", *Reach 96.3 FM*. Accessed July 01, 2020, https://reachfm.ca/christian-news/ christians-at-the-centre-of-coronavirus-outbreak-still-preaching1/.

22. As expected, the government of China did not stay silent, it is now violently cracking down on Christian liberties. See "China orders Christians to destroy crosses on their churches and take down images of Jesus in intensifying crackdown on religion", *Daily Mail (UK)*. Accessed July 22, 2020, https://www.dailymail.co.uk/news/article-8544835/ China-orders-Christians-destroy-crosses-churches-images-Jesus.html/.

Under no circumstances is the great commission ever put on hold, not during pandemics, wars, persecution, recessions, etc. No, on the contrary, Jesus said:

> Go therefore and make disciples of all nations, baptizing them in the name of the Father and of the Son and of the Holy Spirit, teaching them to observe all that I have commanded you. And behold, I am with you always, *to the end of the age* (Matt. 28:19-20).

3. Church is still Important

Last but not least, given the majority of churches across the Americas that had to close their doors due to the lockdowns and restrictions, we need to be reminded of the following fact: "Church is still important." This is, perhaps, a phrase that can be easily misunderstood. I do not mean that we, as Christians, should outright contravene what the government has advised for the health and safety of the public. I am neither advising those considered "high-risk" to venture out where they might be potentially exposed to the coronavirus. What I mean is that: that sacred time of fellowship, of gathering together, of worshiping God in community, *that* must be protected. It may have been tempting (and still is!) to sit back on the couch on a Sunday morning and replace your usual Sunday service with Netflix. But the church, both as an institution and as a collective community, has not "gone on vacation", it never has.

During the lockdowns, many churches sought to honour the governmental authorities that God had set in place by abiding by much of the public health guidelines. Some provided livestreams of their private services, others posted up pre-recorded services on their websites, and there were even those who temporarily ceased their operations until the Fall. But these developments were not without debate. With each passing week there grew a chasm between those who were willing to submit to the state's policies and those who were voicing their protests in hopes of returning to in-person gatherings. The first group, while seeking to be earnest, loyal citizens, were mostly unaware of the growing totalitarian powers of the state and the dangers it posed for religious liberties in the future. The second group were, in fact, better informed, and were involved in various public awareness projects, such as, for example, the organizing of a signed letter and petition that was sent to the premier of Ontario.[23] With the legal threat of a Charter challenge, particularly concerning the violation of religious liberties, it was no surprise that the government yielded.

Even after the provincial government granted permission for churches to gather, with the condition of limiting gatherings to 30% of building capacity, the in-house debates continued given the new guidelines that were introduced, including no singing indoors (no live worship), mask-wearing requirements, amongst other things.[24] The most prominent questions amongst

---

23. Jonathan Pinto, "Hundreds of churches ask premier to let them reopen", *CBC News*. Accessed July 01, 2020, https://www.cbc.ca/news/canada/windsor/hundreds-ontario-churches-ask-reopen-1.5566955/.

24. For a critical reflection on government guidelines and local bylaws as it relates to church operations, see André Schutten and ARPA, "Reflections on the mandatory face mask bylaws

Figure 2: Example of the implementation of a required mask/face-covering by-law by the city of St. Catharines, Ontario, a few weeks before the Region of Niagara followed suit.; Information on COVID-19 and government guidelines are posted on "Coronavirus Disease (COVID-19)", *Government of Canada.* Accessed July 07, 2020, https://www.canada.ca/en/public-health/services/diseases/coronavirus-disease-covid-19.html

churchgoers was: What is the church? Can we be a church without a building? What are the state's limitations in terms of its authority over the church from a biblical perspective? To answer, in brief, the first two questions: the church is both institutional and communal. The church is institutional in the sense that it is structured, there is an authoritative order, there are elders and deacons and members. The church is also communal in the sense that we are a spiritual family spread out across the world, and our worship of God is not confined to what we do in the church building but what we do in the culture. While the church is not defined by a building, per se, it nonetheless must gather to function as an institutional and communal entity. For more on the institutional and communal nature of the church, see Appendix I: What is the Church? As for the third question, the Christian thinkers Aaron Rock and Joseph Boot wrote to the premier of Ontario that:

> the Bible and centuries of tradition oblige Christians to gather weekly for worship and witness around the Word of God and sacraments – we need one another to flourish in our service to Christ (Ex. 20:9-11; 1 Cor. 16:1-2; Heb. 10:24-25; Acts 2:42, 20:7). Neither confessional Christian faith nor the Church institute can faithfully exist without a Lord's Day gathering. This divine obligation and hard-won historic freedom is so important for Christians, that it supersedes all human legislation and regulation. The church is not comparable to a sports

and churches", *Facebook*. Accessed July 23, 2020, https://www.facebook.com/watch/live/?v=328351321506423&ref=watch_permalink/.

or dance club and cannot be dismissed as non-essential by an expert in any field. We would respectfully remind the civil government that the church does not exist by permission of the state, for its establishment and rule is found in Jesus Christ himself.[25]

The church, as God's people, and as His servant, is tasked with ministering the grace of God, while the state, also a servant of God (there is no such thing as a *secular* state, either the state is found to be in obedience or disobedience to God's commands), is tasked with ministering the sword of justice. Both are subject to God, and both have their respective jurisdictions. This is something we can discern in the Old Testament, where the priests (representative of the institution) were not to perform the tasks of the king, and the king was not to perform the tasks of the priests. Both nonetheless were subject to God and His law. This is explained with better clarity by ARPA, the Association of Reformed Political Action:

> Jesus said that we are to "render to Caesar the things that are Caesar's and to God the things that are God's" (Matt. 22:21). The implication is that the church, as an institution, should not direct the affairs of the civil government and vice versa. But this does not mean that faith or religion has no role in the state. It is impossible to make public policy without a moral foundation and direction. The state should protect the place of the church in society so that the church can do its call-

---

25. Aaron Rock and Joseph Boot, "RE: Re-opening Ontario Churches", *Reopen Ontario Churches*. Accessed July 22, 2020, https://www.reopenontariochurches.ca/.

ing which includes equipping its members to honour the state and to function constructively to God's glory within our democracy.[26]

In light of *all* that has taken place, particularly concerning the institutional church and its operations, there has now been a sharply increasing tendency for believers to downplay the importance of church attendance and membership. But we need to take into consideration the following admonishment in the book of Hebrews, not only because they are wise words, but because they are *God's* words:

> And let us consider how to stir up one another to love and good works, not neglecting to meet together, as is the habit of some, but encouraging one another, and all the more as you see the Day drawing near (Heb. 10:24-25).

It is in such times as this that the institutional church must encourage its familial community to continue to gather in order to "stir up one another to love and good works." In fact, believers should be reminding each other continually as to the importance of gathering anew, for we gather to worship our God and King in community, and we gather in order to build each other up so that we can go and live *sent* into the world. As John Piper wrote on the matter:

> Without the ministry of attendance, we cannot be known; if we are not known, we cannot be encouraged; if we are not encouraged, we will not endure. We gather,

26. ARPA, "Core Principles", *ARPA*. Accessed July 22, 2020, https://arpacanada.ca/about-arpa/core-principles/#separation-church-state/.

then, in order to mutually encourage, and we encourage in order to mutually endure. This summons has everything to do with making it to the end: "encouraging one another, and all the more as you see the Day drawing near" (Hebrews 10:25).[27]

While the nation-wide lockdown certainly interrupted our gatherings for a time, it nonetheless brought about something good: a paradigm shift as to how the church can best be ministering to our communities. Consider the words of Jeff Christopherson, the co-founder and missiologist at the SEND Institute, who recently wrote:

> Is God setting us up? Does COVID-19 have broader missiological ramifications? Jesus taught that light was never meant to be contained – but to be on display. This is a concept that we have struggled with as we have competed to 'display' light within our concealing containers… What if we allowed the light to permanently escape our baskets? What if we persisted in organizing for a viral gospel movement? Could the gospel trajectory within North America be affected? Perhaps it is something to consider.[28]

Pandemics have generally changed the world as its moved forward, particularly in regard to healthcare, social interactions, amongst other things; perhaps it will

---

27. John Piper, "The Church Irreplaceable: Why God's People Must Gather", *Desiring God*. Accessed July 22, 2020, https://www.desiringgod.org/articles/the-church-irreplaceable/.

28. Jeff Christopherson, *Twitter*. Accessed March 16, 2020. https://twitter.com/Christopherson3/status/1239179569254617088/.

change how we function *missionally* as a church, both institutionally and communally. We know not what the coming months, years, decades will bring, but we do know that all things are in God's sovereign hands. And irregardless as to what may come, our prayer should always be: "Lord, may the gospel shine brightly in us in this fallen world." There will certainly be no shortage of ministry opportunities before us, may we be found faithful in making the most of them.

APPENDIX

WHAT IS THE
CHURCH?

Addressing the Question

WHAT IS THE CHURCH you ask? Given the multifaceted nature of the church and its functions, that is perhaps one of the most difficult questions for most Christians today to answer correctly. Consider, for example, that if you were to survey the common opinion of believers, you will note that there is an increasing tendency to absolutize one of the many aspects of the church, whether it be defining it solely as a missional agency, a faith-based community, or a socio-religious institution. Just as Christ-followers before us have spilled much ink in trying to articulate a biblical understanding of various doctrines professed by the church, the doctrine *of the church* itself has been no different.[1] While many

---

1. See Millard J. Erickson, *Christian Theology*, Third Edition (Grand Rapids, MI.: Baker Academic, 2013), 950.

theologians have sought to answer this question socio-logically, psychologically, economically, or from some other perspective or discipline, the right step towards answering this question is by asking: What does the Bible teach about the church?

It is one thing to try to define the church from man's limited perspective, it is quite another to define the church according to what God has said in His Word. Our epistemological starting point must not be ourselves. After all, as intelligent as we may think ourselves to be, the *noetic* effects of sin has compromised our capability of perfectly interpreting God's created reality. The late theologian Cornelius Van Til put it this way, as a result of our sinful disposition, we have "made for ourselves a false ideal of knowledge, the ideal of absolute inderivative comprehension."[2] Such an ideal is impossible when you consider that we ourselves, having been created in the image of God, are derivative beings with derivative knowledge. If we seek to understand the church, and to understand it *truly*, we must do so in a way that is different than the way the natural man generally thinks, for according to his impossible ideal he believes himself to be intellectually self-sufficient, radically autonomous, a law unto himself in his own thinking. As a result, our starting point for all knowledge cannot be anything else but God's Word, for being the Creator of the entire cosmos, that which is seen and unseen, His Word is the *only* author-itative interpretation of created reality. It is then, only

2. Cornelius Van Til, *Christian Apologetics*, second edition (Phillipsburg, NJ.: P&R Books, 2003), 42.

by adopting the same presuppositions of Scripture, that can we *truly* know and make sense of, in this case, what the church is.

Having said that, what then can we say in regard to "What is the church?"

An Assembly or Gathering

To beginwith, the Old Testament gives us the Hebrew words *qahal* (לְהָק) and *'edah* (הָדֵע), the former referring to the "summoning of an assembly or congregation" or "the act of assembling", while the latter referring to the "people gathered before the tent of meeting".[3] Why are these particular Hebrew words relevant to our subject matter? Because when these words are translated into the Greek, *qahal* is rendered as *ekklesia* (ἐκκλησία), a Greek term used for the "church", while *'edah* as *sunagógé* (συναγωγή), or "synagogue", which can also, in some circumstances, be used to refer to the church.[4] The predominant word used for the "church" in the New Testament, however, is *ekklesia*, and in regards to how it is employed, it can generally refer to "a group of believers in a specific city" (Acts 5:11; 8:1; 11:22; 12:1, 5; 1 Cor. 1:2; 2 Cor. 1:1; Gal. 1:2; 1 Thess. 1:1; Rev. 1-3), in some cases a group of believers in individual homes (Rom. 16:5; 1 Cor. 16:19; Col. 4:15), or more broadly as "all believers in a given city" or region (Acts 8:1; 9:31; 13:1; 1 Cor. 16:19).[5] To help clarify our understanding of the Greek term *ekklesia*, theologian Millard J. Erickson writes the following:

---

3. Erickson, *Christian Theology*, 955.
4. Ibid., 956.
5. Ibid.

We should note that the individual congregation, or group of believers in a specific place, is never regarded as only a part or component of the whole church. The church is not a sum or composite of the individual local groups. Instead, the whole is found in each place... the individual congregation does not produce the total community or the church. Each community, however small, represents the total community, the church.[6]

Not clear enough? Consider the words of Paul the apostle. When writing his epistles to the Corinthians, he addresses his letters "to the church of God in Corinth" (1 Cor. 1:2; 2 Cor. 1:1). Paul is not writing aimlessly, as if he does not know *who* his audience is; he is consciously addressing the "church" as it is "manifested or appears in one place, namely, Corinth", and as another theologian puts it, though the church "is one throughout the whole world... it is at the same time fully present in every individual assembly."[7] This certainly helps us to understand the church as an assembly, gathering, or congregation, but to be more specific, the church can be understood as a community. Who forms part of this community? God's Word also makes that clear to us: Those who form part of the *ekklesia* are those who are called out by God to be His people. As the apostle Peter writes to the church:

> But you are a chosen race, a royal priesthood, a holy nation, a people for his own possession, that you may

6. Ibid., 957.
7. Ibid., 956-957; Lothar Coenen, "Church" in *The New International Dictionary of New Testament Theology*, Colin Brown, ed. (Grand Rapids, MI.: Zondervan, 1975), 1:291.

proclaim the excellencies of him who called you out of darkness into his marvelous light" (1 Pet. 2:9).

Those whom God calls "His own people" are those who have repented of their sin (Isa. 30:15; Matt. 3:8; 4:17; 21:32; Lk. 5:31-32; 24:46-48; Acts 3:19), placed their trust in the redemptive work of Christ (Rom. 5:8; 6:23; Gal. 6:14; Phil. 2:8; Col. 1:20; 2:14; Heb. 12:2), died to themselves (Mark 8:34; Gal. 2:20), and surrendered their lives to God (Mark 8:35; 10:28; Rom. 12:1). In other words, those who believe in Jesus Christ as their Lord and Saviour, and who exhibit this faith in their lives. But this is only looking at it from one side, that is to say, we are looking at only man's response to the gospel, to the good news of salvation and restoration in Jesus Christ. We must also consider the other side; what God has done in order to make these people *His* people.

The natural man is revealed by Scripture to be dead in his trespasses, dead in his sin (Eph. 2:1; Col. 2:13; 1 Tim. 5:6), he cannot therefore choose life, nor do anything to make himself right again with God. Man is subject to judgment (Eccl. 12:14; Jn. 12:48; Acts 17:31; 2 Cor. 5:10; Heb. 9:27; Rev. 20:11-15). However, the same God who created man in His own image can restore man – beginning first by touching man's heart by the power of His Spirit (Jn. 3:3, 5-8; 6:63; Tit. 3:5; 1 Jn. 5:18), exchanging man's heart of stone for a heart of flesh (Ezek. 36:26). This means to be brought to life, to be born again. And to be born again means that man's will, once enslaved to the power of sin, is liberated. The result of this new life and liberation? Man's new heart, and thus new nature, cannot help but respond to God's grace, His divine unmerited favor (Jn. 5:21; 6:44; 15:16; Acts 16:14; Rom. 8:29-30; Eph. 2:8). However, in order to make man right again, God sent His Son to die on the cross as a sacrificial atonement (Jn. 3:16; Rom. 3:23-26; Heb. 9:28; 10:3-4), as was required by the law, that by fulfilling the law and paying man's sin-debt in full – for the penalty of sin is death (Rom. 6:23) – all those who trust in Christ can be forgiven of their sin and reconciled to God. As Paul writes "you were bought with a price" (1 Cor. 6:20), an immeasurable price, by the grace of God.

The following is what transpires when people are called out by God to be *His* people: they are drawn by the Spirit of God; their hearts, the centrality of their beings, are brought to life and renewed, their sins are forgiven, they are justified in Christ by grace through faith, and they are adopted into the family of God. This redemptive work is not limited to a particular ethnicity – though it began with the people of Israel in the Old Testament, it was always God's plan to open the door of salvation to the whole world. Men and women from all nations and tongues, a beautiful diversity, called together into a homogeneous, integrated unity, the "family of God." To think that once we were slaves to sin, now, having been reconciled with God, we are not treated as mere servants or workers, but we are adopted by Jesus' Heavenly Father as *His* children. In his writing to the Ephesian church, Paul declares this as true: "[God] predestined us for adoption to himself as sons through Jesus Christ, according to the purpose of his will" (Eph. 1:5). In fact, not only are we called "sons" and "daughters" of God, Jesus also calls us His brothers and sisters (Heb. 2:11).

But what about those godly men of faith in the Old Testament? This articulation of God's people is, after all, under the contextual light of the New Testament. Paul also addressed this question when writing to the Roman church. Those whom God had called in the Old Testament, those who had responded in faith to their anticipated salvation and restoration in YHWH and His anointed, also form part of the "family of God" (Rom. 4). They were justified through faith by grace, and therefore, just as those who followed in the New Testament, they were delivered from judgment and reconciled with God. All this God has done to bring forth the church, but with what purpose in mind?

The Threefold Function of the Church

Biblically, the church serves a *threefold* function: (i) to glorify God; (ii) to make the gospel known; and (iii) to make disciples. The Westminster Shorter Catechism states that "Man's chief end is to glorify God (Ps. 86:9; Isa. 60:21; Rom. 11:36; 1 Cor. 6:20; 10:31; Rev. 4:11), and to enjoy him forever (Ps. 16:5-11; 144:15; Isa. 12:2; Lk. 2:10; Phil. 4:4; Rev. 21:3-4)." By this statement the Westminster divines understood that God calls His people to a holistic worship, in which, instead of a privatized religion (which has become prevalent in the West), our faith is expressed as an all-encompassing, comprehensive reality. It logically follows that, if we have received the grace of God for the total renewal of our being, and if we have been restored to our creational purpose in Christ, then we are called to worship and glorify God in all aspects of life. Thus, as grace-bought believers (redeemed by grace), we are to cultivate the comprehensive worship of our lives (and this entails every cultural activity we are involved in) towards the Triune, Creator and Redeemer God of Scripture. As His revealed Word teaches: the church's chief end is to glorify God in all spheres of life and to enjoy Him forever (Gen. 1:28; Ps. 16:5-11; 86; Matt. 28:18-20).

This *first* function of the church, to glorify God, is inseparably linked to its *second* and *third* functions, both of which are considered missional in their nature. In regard to the *second*, "making the gospel known", that is, the work of evangelism, a church that truly glorifies God is a church that is outward turned, that is to say, oriented beyond its four walls. Scripture teaches that, in addition to worshipping God, the church as a community is called to *live out* the gospel in all spheres of life by exhibiting and administering the grace of God (1 Cor. 6:20). This living out of the gospel involves a life that exhibits (i) verbal proclamation, or witnessing of the biblical gospel, (ii) gospel-centred values and (iii) gospel-centred behaviours – that is to say, the cultivation of a culture that manifests godly biblical virtue and pays tribute to the Lordship of Christ. The importance of evangelism cannot be understated in the life of the church; cultural renewal can only possibly follow when there has been heart renewal, and heart renewal can only take place in the context of hearing the gospel.

This is a solemn truth: A church that does not do the work of evangelism is a dead church, for it fails to understand its missional mandate and is instead inward focused as a community. It could even be said, as John Frame puts it, that "it amounts to a repudiation of our Lord's Great Commission",[8] and that is not an offense to be taken lightly. Christ commissioned His people, His church, to make disciples of the nations, this would be an impossibility without evangelism, a *holistic* evangelism. And what is meant is not merely the handing out of tracts and Bibles, but Christian interactions with culture, such as "social action, involvement with the arts, conversations with scientists and philosophers... to reach people and their *culture* for Jesus Christ."[9] It naturally follows that a comprehensive faith would inevitably lead to a grace-filled life, and a grace-filled life cannot but overflow and impact a sinful, broken and fallen world (Matt. 5:13-16; 28:18-20; 1 Cor. 15:24-28).

As I had mentioned "making disciples," this is considered the *third* function of the church. One thing is to have disciples in a church community, as a matter of fact, all believers are disciples. It is quite another thing to *make* disciples. For an understanding of discipleship, the *Lexham Theological Wordbook* defines this task as:

> the process of learning the teachings of Jesus and following after his example in obedience through the

8. John Frame, "A Theology of Opportunity: *Sola Scriptura* and the Great Commission", *Frame-Poythress.* Accessed June 18, 2019, https://frame-poythress.org/a-theology-of-opportunity-sola-scriptura-and-the-great-commission/

9. Ibid.

44 | THE CÁNTARO MONOGRAPHS

power of the Holy Spirit. Discipleship not only involves the process of becoming a disciple but of making other disciples through teaching and evangelism.[10]

The church is thus called to cultivate an informed and faithful community of grace-bought believers impassioned with communicating and embodying God's truth outside the four walls of the church, defending the truth of God's Word in an age of religious confusion, and pursuing Christ in their daily walk for the glory of God (Matt. 28:18-20; 1 Cor. 12:12-27; Heb. 10:25). How is this accomplished? The Greek word *paideia* (παιδεία) provides some insight. When Paul wrote to the Ephesians, he instructed them to raise their children "in the discipline (*paideia*) and instruction of the Lord" (Eph. 6:4). And in his letter to Timothy, Paul stated that Scripture is useful "for training (*paideia*) in righteousness" (2 Tim. 3:16). In the context of Paul's letters, *paideia* means educating for the purpose of discipleship; to educate, to disciple one another in the application and living of God's Word.[11] This fulfillment of *paideia* can only take place in the context of community.

This is the *threefold* function of the church: (i) to glorify God in all spheres of life, (ii) to make known the gospel to all men, and (iii) to disciple one another in God's Word. As we consider the question then, "What

10. C. Byrley, "Discipleship" in *Lexham Theological Wordbook*, eds., D. Mangum, D.R. Brown, R. Klippenstein and R. Hurst (Bellingham, WA.: Lexham Press, 2014).

11. M.S. Robertson, "Discipline" in *Lexham Theological Wordbook*.

is the church?", a contemporary Christian thinker summarized it this way: "In the scriptures the people of God are identified as those who are called out by the Spirit, gathered together as a body and appointed to a task."[12] To be more specific, the inscripturated Word of God describes the church as a missional *community* of grace-bought believers.

Mechanical or Organic Community?

However, in recent years, the nature of the church's "community" has been misconstrued and misunderstood. For some, the church has become nothing more than a non-profit organization, focused solely on social or cultural issues; others have taken it even further and treated it like a business enterprise, producing the cultic movement of the prosperity gospel. There have also been cases in which, because of the church's missional nature, because of its call to make disciples, the church has operated as a mechanical production facility, producing scores of *false* converts, largely due to the emphasis being placed on numbers (how many people *we* can save) as opposed to faithfully testifying and communicating the truth of the gospel.[13] All of these approaches emerge from an epistemological foundation different than Scripture, and thus none of these approaches demonstrate a biblical understanding of the gospel and of the church's "community", as to how it operates. In fact, all these approaches prove

---

12. Joseph Boot, *For Mission: The Need for Scriptural Cultural Theology* (Grimsby, ON.: EICC Publications, 2018), 30.
13. See Ray Comfort, *The Way of the Master* (USA: Bridge-Logos Publishers, 2006).

themselves foreign to the biblical concept of the "family of God" and to the early church of the book of Acts.

What, then, can be said about the nature of this community? We must consult what Scripture teaches. Paul, when writing to the Corinthian church, stated that:

> Just as the body is one and has many members, and all the members of the body, though many, are one body, so it is with Christ. For in one Spirit we were all baptized into one body—Jews or Greeks, slaves or free—and all were made to drink of one Spirit.
>
> For the body does not consist of one member but of many. If the foot should say, "Because I am not a hand, I do not belong to the body," that would not make it any less a part of the body. And if the ear should say, "Because I am not an eye, I do not belong to the body," that would not make it any less a part of the body. If the whole body were an eye, where would be the sense of hearing? If the whole body were an ear, where would be the sense of smell? But as it is, God arranged the members in the body, each one of them, as he chose. If all were a single member, where would the body be? As it is, there are many parts, yet one body.
>
> The eye cannot say to the hand, "I have no need of you," nor again the head to the feet, "I have no need of you." On the contrary, the parts of the body that seem to be weaker are indispensable, and on those parts of the body that we think less honorable we bestow the greater honor, and our unpresentable parts are treated

with greater modesty, which our more presentable parts do not require. But God has so composed the body, giving greater honor to the part that lacked it, that there may be no division in the body, but that the members may have the same care for one another. If one member suffers, all suffer together, if one member is honored, all rejoice together.

Now you are the body of Christ and individually members of it (1 Cor. 12:12-27).

While Paul's exhortation to the Corinthians cannot be clearer, the church in Jerusalem had long before understood this notion of being a community, a family, in Christ (Acts 2:42-47). The rich helped the poor, those with plenty helped those who lacked, and the hungry dined at the same table as those who provided the food. There was *real* care because they *all* understood each other to be brothers and sisters called by the same irresistible grace of God. As the text says: "All the believers were together and had everything in common" (Acts 2:44). This commonality was more than just their profession of faith, as vital and foundational as that proves to be, but also their understanding of the *three-fold* function of the church (Acts 2:42).

Biblical commentator R.C.H. Lenski, when reflecting on the cohesive nature of the body as expressed by Paul, writes that:

As Paul drew each line of the illustration, we felt and saw what he meant in regard to ourselves as members of the church—how natural and right is the proper use of our gifts in harmony with the other members of the body, and, by contrast, how unnatural and wrong are all thoughts and actions that are in conflict with that harmony.[14]

As opposed to seeing the church as an NGO, a business entity, or a mechanical production facility, the church is an *organic* community, a family, a body with many parts, many organs, working collectively towards fulfilling its *threefold* function for the fulfillment of God's will and for His glory alone.

The Familial Structure & Direction of the Church

This concept of an "organic" community, however, is not to suggest that the church is without structure, as some contemporaries have suggested. If there were to be no structure, there would be no church, in the same way that there would be no family. To be "organic" is not to be "fluid", that distinction must be made clear from the very beginning. There is a vast difference between an organic community and a "fluid" entity (the latter is an oxymoron). Can you imagine a family that has no father, mother, son or daughter, brother or sister? And that such concepts were merely social constructs, as our twenty-first century progressivists would like us to believe? That would, of course, be absurd (and yet more people in the West are buying into this!). Or imagine the human body without any definable structure, the supposed "fluidity" that our culture has embraced. What would that make us? A blob? Some abstract entity? Not even that. The moment the

---

14. R.C.H. Lenski, *The Interpretation of St. Paul's First and Second Epistle to the Corinthians* (Minneapolis, MN.: Augsburg Publishing House, 1963), 534.

structural aspect is dismissed, the entity ceases to be. Why? Because God's created order is structural, every creational aspect is structural. Everything in God's created universe, in created reality, is defined by what God created it to be. This is why, the moment you attempt to erase its structural concept and make it something it is not, you are violating God's established creational order. And there are consequences. The progressive family is not a family at all, for how can a family be two fathers, or two mothers, or any number and combination other than God's created order and still be a family? How can two husbands and two wives be considered a marriage? The moment the structure of God's created order is dismissed and violated, decay and corruption invade and threaten to destroy that which was originally declared by God as "good." And it is not just a matter of structure, it is a matter of direction as well. Every structure in God's created universe was built with a particular directional orientation in mind: to glorify God the Creator. The moment man begins to tinker with God's created order and make it into that which it is not, thinking in his own futility that he can reinvent reality, he distorts the direction of whatever he perverts by his own sinful nature, re-orienting it toward glorifying his own radical autonomy.

We are already witnessing this in our day and age: the Western progressivists leading the way to a supposed "utopia", bulldozing over every structural concept, like the family, marriage, human identity, sexuality, etc., rooted in the revelation of God. Why? Because as cultural Marxist thought would have it, the creational order, as revealed and interpreted in God's Word, is too restrictive, it imprisons man from being his true self, whatever he wants and wills to be. Cultural Marxism may as well be a novel development in human history, but radical autonomy is certainly not, it is as ancient as the Garden of Eden. The spirit of the fallen world has always been to fulfill that first and primary sinful desire, to be like gods, to determine for oneself what is real, what is good and evil, and what is known (Gen. 1:1-7). It is the stark contrast, the polar opposite, the antithetical manifestation of the church, God's grace-bought community of believers. And it is that sharp distinction that must not be lost on us. While the world claims to be a plethora of individualized and/or collectivized gods, each doing what is right in his own eyes (Jdg. 21:25), the church, on the other hand, reflects the true structure and direction of human civilization, in which its members are subject in willful obedience to the only true God and His law-word, glorifying the Creator in every sphere of life (1 Cor. 8:5-6).

Consider just how sharp a distinction there is: In no way can we say that the world, as it is alienated from God, operates like a family; each turns to their own way, each plots evil against their own neighbor, the dysfunctional dynamics and disunity make it impossible for the world to be considered a family on an operational/functional level (Gen. 6:5; Isa. 53:6a; Zech. 8:17).[15] The church, however, *IS* a family, its members

15. The only way the world could possibly be considered a family is in the biological sense, as we are all descendants of our first parents, Adam and Eve.

having been called from darkness to light, having been brought from death to life, forgiven and redeemed, adopted into the "family" of Christ by the work of Christ Himself. Again, as Paul had written: "[God] predestined us for adoption to sonship through Jesus Christ, in accordance with his pleasure and will" (Eph. 1:5), and "...because you are sons, God had sent the Spirit of his Son into our hearts, crying, 'Abba! Father!' So you are no longer a slave, but a son, and if a son, then an heir through God" (Gal. 4:6-7). As opposed to the dysfunction, disunity and in-fighting that so characterizes the world and its ways, what is most emphasized and exhibited amongst the grace-bought community of believers is love of God and of our brother and neighbour (Mark 12:30-31). As the nineteenth century Canadian Christian statesman, Sir Oliver Mowat, writes:

> This commandment have we from Him, that he who loveth God do love his neighbour also; we are to love our neighbour as Christ loved all men, and gave himself a sacrifice for them. In discharging this duty we are to bear one another's burdens, and therein fulfill the law of Christ. We are to render glad and loving service in a special sense to the friendless, the sick, the suffering, and the needy, whatever their country or their creed. The Samaritan is to help and do good to the Jew, and the Jew is to help and do good to the Samaritan; Britons to Americans; Americans to Britons. In a word, Christianity enjoins on all to cultivate supreme love to the God and Father of all, and to live towards all men lives of truth, justice, kindness, and active benevolence.

That is what God loves, and requires of us. Without this love on our part, and this goodness of character and conduct towards our fellow men, it is the doctrine of Christianity that the soundness of our faith is nothing—is but as sounding brass and a tinkling cymbal; and is so even though that faith were strong enough as (in the language of the great apostle of the Gentiles) to "remove mountains." It is thus to love, that supreme importance is attached by Christianity.[16]

The love of God *is* love, there is no other love, no matter how many times progressivists want to scream it in the streets with their rainbow-coloured flags, the nature of love, true love, will never be different than the biblical love of God as expressed through the law and his redemptive work. And that love can only originate *from God*. It originates from no one and nowhere else, it is *that* love that is reflected by His grace-bought community of believers, His redeemed and adopted family, sons and daughters of God. It is because of this love that was first bestowed upon us that we can fulfill the *threefold* function of the church, to glorify God in all spheres of life, to make known the gospel to all men, and to disciple one another in the application and living of God's Word.

The church, therefore, has a structure. God revealed this clearly in His Word. It is a missional and purpose-filled grace-bought community "built on the foundation of the apostles and prophets, Christ Jesus himself being the cornerstone" (Eph. 2:20).

---

16. Oliver Mowat, *Christianity and its Influence* (Toronto, ON.: The Hunter, Rose Co., 1898), 18.

In addition to this, there are, as Paul writes, different offices, roles, and authorities within the church:

> And he gave the apostles, the prophets, the evangelists, the shepherds and teachers, to equip the saints for the work of ministry, for building up the body of Christ, until we all attain unity of the faith and of the knowledge of the Son of God, to mature manhood, to the measure of the stature of the fullness of Christ... (Eph. 4:11-13).

The reason as to why these offices were specifically instituted is plainly stated by the apostle Paul, that as a grace-bought community we might (i) be equipped for ministry, (ii) understand true doctrine, and (iii) grow in the grace and knowledge of the Lord Jesus Christ unto full maturity (vv. 12-13; see also 2 Pet. 3:18). While these were certainly specialized offices, the latter three of which have carried on to today, the nature of these offices also communicates a general calling for the church. How so? The Greek *apostolos* (ἀπόστολος), for example, means "one sent on a mission". Given that the church can be understood as God's "sent ones", the apostolic calling of the church is to be God's missional people, sent out into the world to make the gospel known and to minister the grace of the gospel in all spheres of life. Or consider the "prophetic" calling of the church, God's prophets were not your run-of-the-mill soothsayers, predicting the future like fortune-tellers. No, they were God's messengers delivering encouragement, exhortation and correction, and sometimes this involved prophecy of events to come. The church, as a collective community, can partake in and fulfill this prophetic calling today by the exposition, proclamation and application of God's Word, and this includes confronting sin not only within the church, but in the public square as well. The same can be said about the other offices, in that, just as the church has an apostolic and prophetic calling, so too does it have an evangelistic, pastoral and tutorial calling.[17]

Also worthy of consideration is that amongst the five offices mentioned by the apostle Paul, one is expanded on – that of the elders, who are responsible for the primary leadership and oversight of the church (1 Tim. 3:1-16) – and one is added – that of the deacons, who are responsible for providing practical service and help in the life of the church (Acts 6:1-6; 1 Tim. 3:8-13). In terms of what the elders are tasked with, Alexander Strauch, in his book *Biblical Eldership*, writes that:

> Elders lead the church (1 Tim. 5:17; Tit. 1:7; 1 Pt. 5:1-2), teach and preach the Word (1 Tim. 3:2; 2 Tim. 4:2; Tit. 1:9), protect the church from false teachers (Acts 20:17, 28-31), exhort and admonish the saints in sound doctrine (1 Tim. 4:13 2 Tim. 3:13-17; Tit. 1:9), visit the sick and pray (Jam. 5:14; Acts 6:4), and judge doctrinal issues (Acts 15:6). In biblical terminology, elders shepherd, oversee, lead and care for the local church.[18]

---

17. See David Robinson and Joseph Boot, "The Church and our Calling Sermon Series", *Ezra Institute for Contemporary Christianity*. Accessed June 13, 2019, https://www.ezrainstitute.ca/resource-library/series-index/the-church-and-our-calling/.

18. Alexander Strauch, *Biblical Eldership: An Urgent Call to Restore Biblical Church Leadership* (Colorado Springs, CO.: Lewis & Roth Publishers, 1995), 16.

A mistaken distinction is sometimes made between pastor and elder, but biblically these are one and the same office given that elders are to both shepherd God's flock (1 Pet. 5:1-2) and exercise pastoral duties (Acts 20:28). As for deacons, from the Greek *diakon-*, they are to serve the church by providing assistance with respect to the basic necessities of life (Matt. 4:11 8:15; 27:55; Lk. 10:40; Rom. 15:25), which includes food, drink, and clothing. Because of the nature of their servanthood, they are also specially tasked with providing hospitality and welcoming.

There is yet more, which although are not particular offices, are nonetheless roles that can be fulfilled in the community of the church, such as older woman teaching younger women "to love their husbands and children, to be self-controlled, pure, working at home, kind, and submissive to their own husbands, that the word of God may not be reviled" (Tit. 2:3-5). By the words "working at home", Paul means to say being productive and an overseer of the home; the woman from Proverbs 31 comes to mind. Likewise, older men are to teach younger men "to be self-controlled" and "sound in faith, in love and in endurance" (Tit. 2:2, 6). It could better be said that these roles are a fulfillment of the church's tutorial calling, with some overlap with its prophetic and pastoral callings.

What about the Church as an Institution?

At this point we can already begin to see why in some cases the church can be referred to as an institution, and why in other cases, as a familial community. The church appears to provide the impression that it is both. This is not wrong, to be precise. In fact, in one sense the church can be understood as an institution, but not in its entirety, it is not entirely an institution, rather, the instituted church is part of the greater functioning organism. Abraham Kuyper, in his *Encyclopedia of Sacred Theology: Its Principles*, provides some clarity on this matter:

> The conception of the instituted Church [or the church as an institution] is much narrower than the Church of Christ when taken as the body of Christ, for this includes in itself all the powers and workings that arise from re-creation. There is a Christian disposition and a Christian fellowship, there is a Christian knowledge and a Christian art, etc., which indeed spring from the field of the Church and can flourish on this field alone, but which by no means therefore proceed from the instituted Church. The instituted Church finds her province bounded by her *offices*, and these offices are limited to the ministry of the Word, the Sacraments, Benevolence, and Church government... All other expressions of Christian life do not work by the organ of the special offices, but by the organs of the re-created natural life; the Christian family by the believing father and mother, Christian art by the believing artist, and Christian schools by the believing magister.[19]

By this we can say that, while the church can be referred to as an institution, the church is more than just an institution, the instituted church is part of the

---

19. Abraham Kuyper, *Encyclopedia of Sacred Theology: Its Principles*, trans. J. Hendrik De Vries (New York: Charles Scribner's Sons, 1898), 587-588.

greater organism of the body of Christ, the family of God.[20] Thus, when we consider this truth, and when we reconcile these various offices, callings, roles, and their accompanying responsibilities for fulfilling the *threefold* function and purpose of the church, along with that which is manifested beyond the institution of the church, such as the Christian's work in different aspects of life as a result of gospel renewal (as referred to by Kuyper), we see how the church is a structurally organized *family* – not a business, not a non-profit organization, not a social club – a divinely instituted structured family, directionally oriented towards glorifying God our Creator and Redeemer.

After all, when the Bible pervasively uses such *familial* terms for God's people, how are we not to understand the church if not in terms of a family? John Calvin, for example, wrote when citing the patristic Cyprian that "to those to whom [God] is a Father, the Church must also be a mother."[21] He understood it, the familial nature of those called out of the world into union and fellowship with Christ and with each other. It is this family of grace-bought believers that will inevitably grow as God continues to draw the nations unto Himself, and the resulting culture cultivated by

---

20. The Dutch philosopher Andree Troost (1916-2008) stated that "To say that the institutional church represents the total community of all believers is tantamount to absolutizing the church on earth" in Troost, *What is Reformational Philosophy?* (Jordan Station, ON.: Paideia Press, 2012).

21. John Calvin, *The Institutes of the Christian Religion*, translated by Henry Beveridge (Peabody: Hendrickson Publishers, 2008), 4.1.1.

those who have been called out to be God's people will permeate the world until all things are made subject to Christ (1 Cor. 15:24-28). That is exactly what Kuyper meant by the work of "the organs of the re-created natural life."[22]

The church was brought forth by God, for the fulfillment of the will of God, for the advancement of the kingdom of God, for the glory of God. No one can relegate the church to the cultural sidelines as some religious community of privatized pietism, and no one can reduce the church to some absolutized aspect or distortion of its multi-faceted functions. The church will always be the church according to the Word of God.

---

22. Kuyper, *Encyclopedia of Sacred Theology*, 588.

ABOUT THE AUTHOR

Steven R. Martins is the founding director of the Cántaro Institute and founding pastor of Sevilla Chapel in St. Catharines, Ontario, Canada. A second-generation Canadian, Steven is of Ibero-American parentage and has worked in the fields of missional apologetics and church leadership for several years. He has spoken at numerous conferences, churches, and University student events, from York University, Toronto, to the University of West Indies in Port of Spain, Trinidad, and the national Universities of Costa Rica (UNCR and UNC), and the Evangelical University of El Salvador. He has also contributed articles to Coalición por el Evangelio (TGC in Spanish) and the *Siglo XXI* journal of Editorial CLIR.

Steven holds a Master's degree *summa cum laude* in Theological Studies with a focus on Christian apologetics from Veritas International University (Santa Ana, CA., USA) and a Bachelor of Human Resource Management from York University (Toronto, ON., Canada). Steven has served on the executive board for Answers in Genesis Canada, and has served in the past with the Ezra Institute for Contemporary Christianity (EICC) as a staff apologist, writer and director of ministry development and advancement (DMDA) for four years. He has also served pastorally at Harbour Fellowship Church in St. Catharines. Steven is married to Cindy and lives in Niagara with their two children.

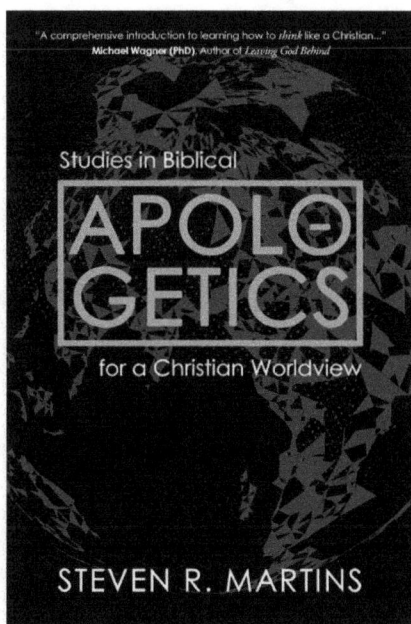

"A comprehensive introduction to learning how to *think* like a Christian..."
Michael Wagner (PhD), Author of *Leaving God Behind*

Studies in Biblical

APOLⓞGETICS

for a Christian Worldview

STEVEN R. MARTINS

"Faithful to the *cosmic* nature and scope of the gospel, the apologetic mandate is a *holistic* defense of the Christian philosophy of life."

Steven R. Martins

COMING 2021